To:
Ed & Janna
From: Lisa Howard
Feb. 1993
(Baby Shower Gift)

This book belongs to

Bronwyn Rhiannon

Charlie Parker
played
be bop

Chris Raschka

ORCHARD BOOKS NEW YORK

Orchard Books, 95 Madison Avenue, New York, NY 10016

Manufactured in the United States of America. Printed by Barton Press, Inc.
Bound by Horowitz/Rae. Book design by Mina Greenstein.
The text of this book is set in Caslon 540 and Helvetica condensed. The illustrations are watercolor and charcoal pencil, reproduced in full color.

10   9   8   7   6   5   4   3   2

Library of Congress Cataloging-in-Publication Data
Raschka, Christopher. Charlie Parker played be bop / by Chris Raschka.   p.   cm. Summary: Introduces the famous saxophonist and his style of jazz known as bebop.
ISBN 0-531-05999-5.   ISBN 0-531-08599-6 (lib. bdg.)
1. Parker, Charlie, 1920–1955—Juvenile literature.   2. Jazz musicians—United States—Biography—Juvenile literature.   [1. Parker, Charlie, 1920–1955.   2. Musicians.   3. Jazz.   4. Afro-Americans—Biography.]   I. Title.   II. Title: Charlie Parker played bebop.   ML3930.P24R4   1992
788.7'3165'092—dc20   [B]   91-38420

To Phil Schaap

Charlie Parker played be bop.

Charlie Parker played **saxophone.**

The music sounded like be bop.

Never leave your cat alone.

Be bop.

Fisk, fisk.

Lollipop.

Boomba, boomba.

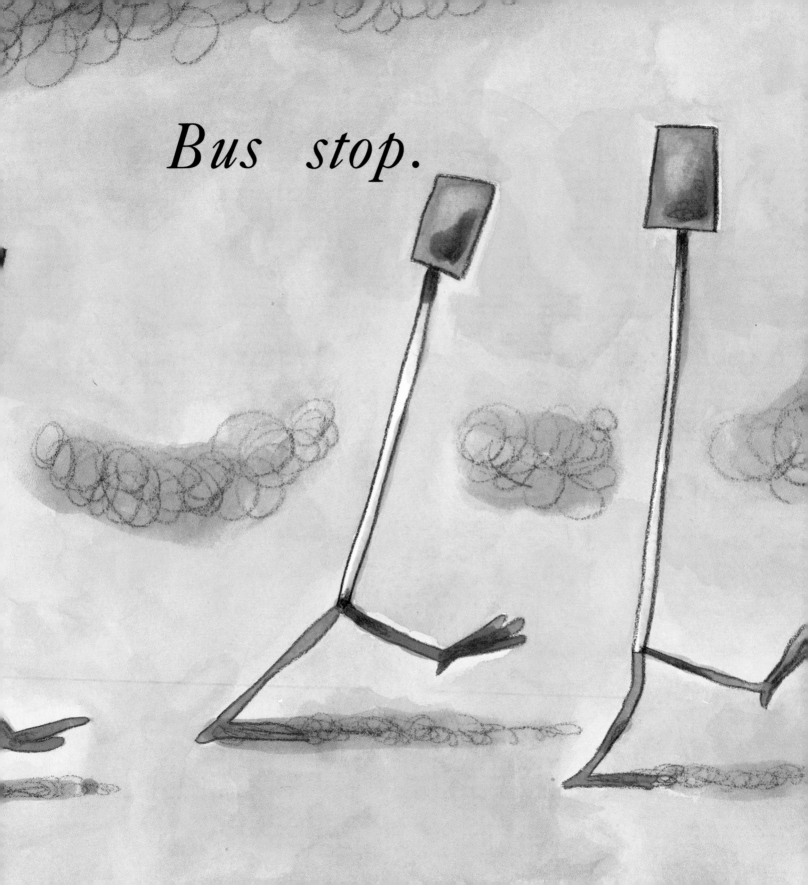

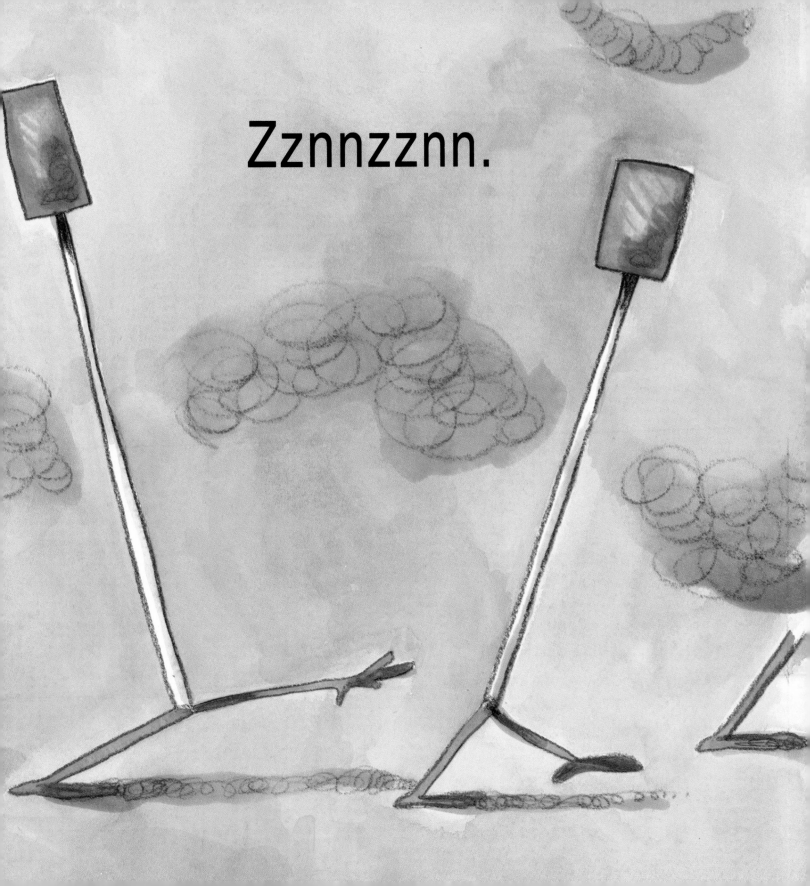

Boppitty, bibbitty,

Charlie Parker played **be bop.**

Charlie Parker played **no trombone.**

The music sounded like be bop.

Barbeque that last leg bone.

Alphabet, alphabet, alphabet, alph,

Chickadee, chickadee, chickadee, chick,

Overshoes, overshoes, overshoes, o,

Reeti-footi, reeti-footi, reeti-footi, ree.

Charlie Parker played be bop.

Charlie Parker played alto saxophone.

The music sounded like hip hop.

Never leave your cat . . .

a-  lone.